How to Win in Workers' Compensation Court

A Practical Guide
From Personal Experience

By

Raymond Hall

WIN IN WORKERS' COMPENSATION COURT

How to Win in Workers' Compensation Court

A Practical Guide
From Personal Experience

This publication is intended to provide practical information from personal experience, regarding the subject matter covered. It is sold with the understanding that the author and publisher are not engaged in rendering legal, accounting, medical or other professional services. If legal or financial advice, or other expert assistance, is required the services of a competent professional person should be acquired.

Copyright © 2018 by Raymond L. Hall

Printed in the United States of America.

Description

This book is a practical guide to help you win in Workers Compensation court. I have personal experience with Workers Compensation due to a work-related lower back injury I suffered while lifting a heavy load into a dump truck. I had to defend my case before a Workers Compensation judge.

Topics included in this book are: injury, disability, accident, depositions, medical records, doctor, disfigurement, pharmacy, investigation, diary, exercise, deposition, cortisone, nerve block, traction, weather, eyewitness, photograph, letters, lost wages, money issues, stress, retraining, medication, therapy, surgery, recovery, physical limitations, pain, suffering, back brace, heating pad, records, fear, worker, workers, workman, occupation, industrial, lifting, chemicals, negligent, insurance, safety, wheelchair, claim, documentation, hospital, ambulance, evidence, diagnosis, X-ray, MRI, CT Scan, myelogram, orthotic, rules, healing, mental, emotional, self-worth, and life after injury.

This book will benefit the injured worker, family members, friends, and anyone you know that needs help resolving the consequences of a work-related injury.

Thank you for purchasing this book.

Please leave a favorable customer review comment on Amazon about this book.

Table of Contents

Introduction

What causes work-related injuries?

The answers can be limitless, but the usual reasons involve material handling; lifting heavy objects, slips, trips and falls; being struck by or colliding with an object; accidents involving tools; and traumas occurring over time due to overuse of a body part or severe strain. Other reasons may include exposure to hazardous chemicals or metals and hearing loss.

My story goes something like this:

- I was injured at work lifting a very heavy piece of machinery into a high dump truck. The company did not provide heavy lifting equipment for the job, but they should have.

- Our boss said we were young and muscular and didn't need the lifting equipment, so a few co-workers and I loaded that damaged machinery into the dump truck.

- The result was a permanent injury to my lower back.

- I was absent from work for six weeks, under doctors care, took numerous medications, had multiple diagnostic tests, and received therapy before returning to work.

- Over the next few years, I aggravated my back at work numerous times shoveling snow, lifting heavy objects, repairing machinery, climbing ladders, and painting.

- Every time I aggravated my back I was absent from work for weeks.

- Eventually, I was transported to the hospital from work by ambulance. My doctor said I could not return to my job because the damage to my back was too severe.

If you are reading this book, perhaps you have experienced a similar situation.

If your injury happened on the job, your employer should provide you with an Employer's Report of Injury form. The form notifies the Workers Compensation Board of your injury. You must complete the form and mail it to the address provided.

The Workers Compensation Board should send you a Notice to Claimant form. This form acknowledges that the Workers Compensation Board received your Report of Injury form and created a file in connection with your injury.

Your employer should send an Employer's Report of Injured Employee's Change of Employment Status Resulting From Injury form to the Workers Compensation Board. This form documents the injury and date, nature of the injury, days missed from work, the employer's address and employer's insurance carrier.

These forms begin the process of communicating with the Workers Compensation Board. The process may be frustrating at times. Responding to the board is even more difficult when you are in pain and possibly immobile. You must complete the forms and respond to the phone calls promptly. It doesn't matter if you are in the hospital, frequently visiting doctors, going to therapy, and taking powerful painkillers.

In addition to responding to Workers Compensation demands, an injured person may be experiencing extreme stress from unpaid bills and an uncertain future. This book will help you conquer the bureaucratic process by educating yourself, organizing your records, and meticulously documenting your case. When you face the Workers Compensation judge at your hearing, your chances for a positive outcome will be significantly enhanced.

You may walk a little slower or find it difficult to stand for long periods. You may have to give up some physically demanding activities that you enjoyed, like playing softball, cutting firewood, or skiing. Part of the healing process involves acknowledging your limitations, accepting them, and focusing on the things you can do. Your life is not over, and your contributions to your family have not ended.

You may need to retrain for a new occupation. Be willing to accept the advice of others, be open to new ideas, take advantage of retraining opportunities, and consider being more reliant on a spouse, or someone else, to help provide for your family. You still have value and a purpose. Let the healing begin.

What is Workers' Compensation?

The Worker's Compensation Act grew out of the Industrial Revolution as a pact between employees and their employers. Workers injured on the job, or who contracted occupational diseases, surrendered their right to sue their employer. They were promised appropriate medical care and a salary while they were out of work. If unable to return to work they received disability payments or vocational rehabilitation.

Workers' compensation legislation was first passed in Germany, Austria, and Great Britain in the late 1800s. By 1920 all but six states in the U.S. had passed some form of Workers Compensation law. Now every state participates, and 85% of U.S. workers are covered by Workers Compensation laws and states' insurance plans. To encourage employers to carry Workers' Compensation insurance, the Acts eliminate employees' rights to bring legal action directly against their employer. Generally, Workers' Compensation pays for medical costs and lost wages only.

The laws created ranges of payment for accidental injuries that occurred on the job. It doesn't matter if the employee or the employer is responsible for the accident. Coverage varies when it comes to benefits paid for death, total disability, or partial disability. Accidents must be reported to a compensation board that grants awards to injured workers or, in case of death, to their families. Recently, states have provided coverage for occupational diseases

Employers have agreed to educate their employees about workplace safety issues and provide methods to prevent injuries. Employers are rewarded with lower insurance premiums. State programs vary substantially. Generally, all Workers' Compensation programs provide the following benefits:

- Cash payment for lost wages

- Death benefits for dependent survivors, including some income support and funeral and burial expenses

- Medical and rehabilitation expenses

- Partial or total disability benefits for temporary or permanent disabilities

- These benefits DO NOT include any payment for pain and suffering

Employer paid insurance plans pay all applicable expenses incurred by an employee injured at work. Rates are based on industry classification groups and claims. While some states mandate insurance coverage through their state agency, others allow employers to purchase private insurance or self-insure. A small number of states allow employers the option to be non-subscribers to Workers' Compensation.

If you are injured on the job you will be required to attend one, and possibly several, hearings before the Workers Compensation Board for your State and County. Usually, at the first hearing, you will testify under oath as to the circumstances of your injury and disability. The judge, a Workers' Compensation insurance carrier representative, and your employer's insurance company representatives will question you. Normally, less than thirty minutes is required to review your testimony.

As the injured person, you are the claimant. Co-workers who witnessed the accident or injury may testify at the first hearing or may be interviewed during a deposition. Eventually, depositions from your doctor, the Workers Compensation doctors, and the insurance company's doctor will be presented. At a later hearing, your employer may present non-medical witnesses to testify on their behalf.

After all the evidence is presented, the case will be closed. The Judge's decision is prepared and mailed to you, possibly several months after the hearing.

An appeal can be filed with the Worker's Compensation Appeal Board. However, the Judge is the final finder of facts. Factual issues cannot be overturned on appeal.

Winning in Workers' Compensation Court

To win in Workers' Compensation Court, you need facts, statistics, documentation, and the general appearance that you are in control. You cannot sue an employer that carries Workers' Compensation insurance, but evidence of wrongdoing or negligence by your employer can tip the scales in your favor during Compensation Court. Whether you hire an attorney or not, you can benefit from this guide.

Your Personal Files

1.   Establish a personal filing system immediately. You will be inundated with forms, letters and doctor bills.

- Buy a three-ring notebook and file all your documentation in it.

- File papers neatly by their date so they are easy to locate when you are in court. Make tabs for each month initially, then for each year, and file your paperwork behind the appropriate tab.

- Punch and file every piece of paper that you receive from your employer's insurance carrier, your state Workers' Compensation office, your doctors, and your employer.

- Keep copies of all letters or forms that you send to, or receive from, Workers' Compensation.

- File this guide in your notebook as a reference document.

2. Document the events surrounding the original accident, injury or illness while they are fresh in your mind.

    - Acquire photographs of the room, area, or machinery involved.

    - Get eyewitness accounts, if possible, in writing.

    - Document significant events that may have contributed to your injury or illness. Examples include: "that week I worked 10 hours overtime, unloaded an eighteen-wheeler full of lumber, stacked a load of cinder blocks, and cleaned out the garage at work. No back support was provided."

    - Keep a daily diary of how you feel, the pain you experience, the location of the pain, the intensity of the pain on a scale of 1-10, the time of day, and what brought the pain on (if anything specifically).

    - Write down things that you cannot do since the injury or illness occurred.

    - Take photographs of your injuries if possible. Physical evidence like scoliosis in your back, bruises on your face, or scars should be documented with photos and dated.

3.   Go to the library and do research:

- Learn everything you can about your medical condition.

- If unusual weather conditions contributed to your injury or illness, you need evidence for your records. Your local newspaper's weather reports contain documentation of heavy snowfalls, extreme heat, extreme cold, high winds, thunderstorms, and lightning. Your local library should have a collection of the newspapers.

- The National Oceanic and Atmospheric Administration (NOAA) can also be a great help with climatological data and statistics.

- If you feel that your employer was negligent, you should document the issues. Get facts about labor laws and research your employer's record. Look for a history of previous violations.

- Obtain data about critical pieces of evidence, such as the exact weight of the boxes of paper you were lifting when you hurt your back, or the chemicals you were exposed to at your job and their side effects. Material Safety Data Sheets (MSDS) explain the dangers of chemicals (like toluene, methyl ethyl ketone, ammonia, or acetone) and are available for every chemical on the market and must be on file for chemicals used by your employer.

4.   Acquire your prior medical records from your
        family doctor. Acquire military medical records if
        applicable. These will document any pre-existing
        conditions that you had or didn't have, before the
        accident. They will also document your pre-injury,
        or pre-illness, height, weight, and general physical
        condition. Over time, a serious injury or illness can
        affect your body in ways that you would not
        anticipate; i.e., discovering a year after a serious
        lower back injury that you lost an inch in height.

5.   Document each medication prescribed to you, the
        side effects of the medication and the length of time
        you take it. Keep the labels from the empty bottles
        and attach them to a sheet of paper in your
        notebook. If you develop other health problems,
        such as kidney or liver damage, you may be able to
        prove it was a result of the medication your doctor
        prescribed. It is best to take any medication only as
        prescribed and only when needed. Most
        medications have some adverse side effects.

Samples of Personal Journal Entries

It is imperative that you keep a journal from the day of your injury, and even the events leading up to your injury until Workers' Compensation makes a final decision. A day planner helps to document events with their appropriate day. Or use a notebook or the computer to keep a running log of your appointments, episodes, treatments, feelings, etc. Here are some samples of the types of things you may include in your journal.

- I unloaded two moving vans full of furniture into the building and rooms (Dec 27).

- I shoveled snow for at least two hours every day this week (Jan 14-21).

- I moved heavy equipment all day (Feb 1).

- I was hospitalized, received traction, therapy, medication, myelogram, CAT scan, cortisone nerve block (Feb 18).

- I acquired documentation from the National Weather Service that we had a record-breaking, 100-year snowfall this winter (document added to my file) (Apr 4).

- I can't bend over far enough to tie my shoes (Apr 5).

- I went home from work with severe back pain (Apr 14).

- I was 5'8-1/2 inches tall ten years ago per my military records. Now I am only 5'7" tall (May 20).

- I located my military driver's license copied it for my records (Aug 6).

- It is painful to get into and out of my car (May 29).

- I returned to work (May 31).

- I had to get an ultrasound treatment to continue working. I have a sore spot in the small of my back the size of a half-dollar (June 7).

- I had a doctor appointment and was fitted for a back support corset. I can't bend over and touch my toes without pain. I was prescribed pain medication and muscle relaxers. (June 16).

- I went to Back School to learn exercises for my back (July 12).

Sample Prescription Drug Ledger

Date Purchased	Prescription Drug	Cost	Date Reimbursed by Workers' Compensation
4/17/xx	Soma Compound xxmg	$65.00	6/5/xx
4/17/xx	Nalfon xxmg	$56.50	6/5/xx
4/17/xx	Tylenol #3 xxmg	46.74	6/5/xx

Sample Letter to Workers' Compensation Office

Workers' Compensation Office
State Office Building
1234 Main Street
Anytown, State 98765

Month, Day, Year

Reference: Insurance carrier claim number: 1234-567
            Workers' Compensation Board claim
number: 7654 3210
            Your social security number: xxx-xx-xxxx

Subject: Reimbursement for Prescription Medication
Charges

I have contacted you on numerous occasions within the last few months without any response. My Workers' Compensation case is very well established and verified. The details of my accident have been meticulously defined in letters sent to you by registered mail, dated 12/30/xx, 4/4/xx, and 12/3/xx.

The last check I received from you was for $11.87 on March 14, xxxx. I have sent receipts for over $211.00 since that time and have not been reimbursed one dime. I owe Best Pharmacy over $500.00 (statement attached) and am very concerned about this indebtedness. They have demanded a substantial payment before I can make any further charges.

I am hereby requesting a hearing regarding this matter. Copies of this letter and my previous letters will be mailed to State Senator Rogers.

As you can guess I am very frustrated with being in constant pain, being deprived of a quality life, and being denied prompt reimbursement of medical expenses from a work-related injury. The laws are in place, the insurance coverage is in place, and the case is well established and convincingly documented as legitimate --- yet the system is not functioning efficiently.

Thank you for your prompt assistance in this matter.

Sincerely,

Signature _____

Full Name _____

Address _____

Cc: XYZ Insurance Company
State Senator Rogers
My Personal File

Workers' Compensation Office Communications

1. Write a letter to your Workers' Compensation representative explaining your viewpoint of what happened. Send them copies of your supporting evidence, your documentation, and show them that you are keeping good records.

2. Mail everything that you send to Workers' Compensation via Certified Mail, so you have proof that you sent it and proof that they received it. Keep the receipts in your notebook.

3. Reference your claim numbers and social security number on every piece of correspondence that you send to the insurance carrier and Workers' Compensation.

4. Photocopy all checks that you receive from your employer's insurance carrier or Workers' Compensation before you cash them. Save the copies in your notebook.

5. You may be scheduled for an examination by a Workers' Compensation doctor. You should be reimbursed for round-trip travel mileage to the doctor's office.

6. You may be asked to give a deposition (an oral questioning session in your home or over the telephone) by Workers' Compensation or by your employer's insurance carrier. Your conversation will be recorded, and you should request a written

copy of the deposition for your files. Be sure to ask a friend or relative to be present as a witness during the deposition. Make sure that what you say during your deposition is consistent with what you say at the Workers' Compensation hearing. Any inconsistencies could be used against you.

7.   There is more to a Workers' Compensation claim than doctor bills and prescriptions. Remind them of the human suffering, the fears you are experiencing, the family stress, the marital stresses, the parental duties you can't perform, and the homeowner's chores that aren't getting done. Be specific and honest, as in the following examples:

- "I can't play ball with son since the accident."

- "My compact car is impossible to get into or out of without pain since the accident."

- "I can't sit through a church service since the accident, because of pain."

- "I had to hire a handyman to perform minor maintenance to our home since the accident."

- "I don't sleep through the night because of pain."

Workers' Compensation needs to be reminded that they are dealing with a person, a spouse, and a parent. You are not just a number and a name.

It is doubtful that you will receive money for "pain and suffering." Generally, Workers' Compensation pays for medical costs and lost wages only. However, the pain and suffering you experience should be documented and forwarded to them as evidence to tip the scales in your favor.

8. Keep communicating with the Workers' Compensation office and their insurance carriers.

    - Write letters to them whenever you have questions, concerns, etc. Phone calls are hard to document after the fact. Letters work to your advantage.

    - Keep your name and your situation fresh in their minds. To them, you are just a number, among zillions of other numbers. Send them a picture of yourself if you wish, so they have a face to put with the number and name.

    - Be courteous, but firm. Never lie to Workers' Compensation. Arm yourself with facts, details, and statistics, so your situation doesn't sound insignificant.

    - Ask them for information about occupational retraining and rehabilitation. Workers' Compensation should pay for it.

- Ask what happens if you experience a re-occurrence of symptoms or you re-injure yourself after returning to work.

- Ask for assistance in paying for services that you used to perform yourself.

- Tell them if you need unique items like a ramp to your front porch, a wider door to your bathroom, a hospital-type bed, or a van with a wheelchair lift.

- Tell them if your doctor says you have to lose weight, but you need the help of a professional weight loss center and can't afford it.

- Remind them that you cannot do the things you did before the injury or illness.

- Remind them that you are still experiencing pain, even though you may have gotten used to it and have learned to live with it.

- Tell them if you need therapy the help heal from your injury.

- Let them know that you are keeping meticulous files regarding your case.

- Don't let them lose you in their paperwork shuffle. They are dealing with thousands of cases and are probably understaffed. Stay in touch and make them reply to you.

9.   Notify Workers' Compensation and the insurance carrier if you intend to move, change jobs, or make any significant change in your situation. They need your current address to communicate with you.

10.   If Workers' Compensation offers you a cash settlement be very cautious. Once you accept the money, you may not be able to re-open the case if the symptoms worsen. It may be better for you to let them pay all your related medical expenses for the rest of your life. Get professional advice, or gather all the facts yourself, and then weigh the pros and cons before deciding. You may have good family medical insurance coverage now, through your spouse or otherwise, but you may not have it in five years. And in cases where insurance companies will not pay for pre-existing conditions, future medical expenses connected with your work-related injury would have to come out of your pocket.

Your Doctor and Pharmacist

1.   Keep records of all doctor visits, prescription drugs prescribed, physical therapy treatments, hospital stays, x-rays, CT scan results, MRI results, etc. Obtain copies of your doctor's records related to your case. Photocopy them before you give them to your employer. Keep all copies and documentation in chronological order in your notebook.

2.   If you need items like a back brace, cane, heating pad, whirlpool device, crutches, ace bandages, heat

packs, etc. ask your doctor to write prescriptions for them so that Workers' Compensation will pay for them.

3.   Ask your pharmacist to provide you with monthly reports of all prescriptions written and filled which relate to your Workers' Compensation claim. Some pharmacists will bill Workers' Compensation claims directly, so you don't have to prepay.

4.   Keep copies of any notes your doctor or therapist issues to you. Even though these are meant to give to your employer or insurance carrier, always keep a copy for your files. These may include statements like:

- "Remain off work until next appointment."

- "Lower back pain- injured moving equipment in the garage- no work for one week."

- "Received Ultra Sound treatment on the lower back."

- "May return to work on x/xx/xx."

- "Off work today due to back problems. Remain off work and avoid standing until 01/01/19xx."

- "Avoid lifting over 25 pounds."

Creditors and Personal Insurance Companies

1. Many financial institutions provide disability insurance or special arrangements for loan payments while customers are not working due to a disabling injury or serious illness. Contact every bank or loan agency that you do business with and inform them that you cannot work.

2. Check all of your insurance policies for disability coverage. Don't forget policies that are provided through your employer and paid for by payroll deduction. Also check car insurance, insurance through banks and credit unions, and any other insurance coverage you have and look for special considerations for disabilities or inability to work.

Communicating With Elected Officials

1. Write to your state congressmen, senators and other political representatives if you get frustrated with the Workers' Compensation system. They may be of help. If they do help you, don't forget to send them a thank you letter. My state senator helped me get reimbursed for prescription drugs after a long battle with the Workers' Compensation insurance carrier.

Workers' Compensation Court Hearing

1. When ordered to appear before a Workers' Compensation hearing or Claims Court follow these principles of success:

    - Make a neat and organized list of questions. Include details and facts that you want the judge to hear while you have his attention. Remember that the entire hearing will be recorded by a court stenographer and will become an official record in your file.

    - Mark your notebook so you can find information quickly without rustling numerous papers to get an answer. Be prepared, be organized, don't get caught saying "I have that paperwork, but I can't find it right now." Take your notebook with you to the hearing.

    - Over-prepare for the hearing. Anticipate the arguments from the insurance carrier and the Workers' Compensation office. Don't let yourself get caught off guard at the hearing because you won't get a second chance to defend yourself. Rehearse your presentation several times before the day of the hearing.

    - Get a haircut and dress as professionally as possible for the hearing. Arrive early to the hearing and get familiar with the room and the surroundings.

- Take or wear any medical devices prescribed for your condition. These items include, but are not limited to, crutches, canes, walkers, back braces, slings, wrist supports, and oxygen.

- Try not to take medications that make you drowsy before the hearing. You need to be as alert as possible.

- Be assertive during the hearing and make sure all your questions are answered and all your concerns voiced. Request written copies of everything agreed on in the hearing.

- Act confident and prepared. Don't get mad, don't swear, don't yell at the judge, and don't lose your temper. Act respectful and professional. You are in a courtroom, and the judge is in charge and must be respected. Thank the judge, and the other representatives present, when your hearing is over.

- The insurance representative and the Workers' Compensation representative are NOT anxiously waiting to give you everything you want. You have to defend yourself, voice your concerns, and convince the judge to order the insurance carrier and Workers' Compensation representative to comply with your wishes.

- The judge needs to see you as someone worth retraining - intelligent, skilled, talented or at least showing lots of potential.

Conquering Fear

A disabling injury can be one of the most fearful events a person will experience. Thoughts like "will this pain ever go away?", or "will I ever work again?", or "how will these bills get paid?", or "will my spouse want me if I am disabled?" are common fears of people who have had serious injuries. The encouraging news is that the pain will diminish and probably go away completely. Advances with pain management, pain relief, orthotics, and prosthetics are encouraging.

If you cannot return to your old job, retraining may provide you with new skills that you can perform with your physical limitations. Also, with the abundance of computers in the workplace and homes it is possible to work at home and send the work to your employer using a modem or fax machine.

Your creditors will reduce your monthly payments if you discuss your situation with them. If necessary, consult a financial consultant to assist in getting a handle on your finances.

The important thing to remember is that your life still has value. Focus on the things you can do, not on the things you can't do. Your situation has changed, your life will be different, there will be adjustments, and you will need to learn new skills. But, you can lead a productive life if you give yourself half a chance, work hard, and keep an open mind.

The biggest battle you will fight is the one in your head. If you remain positive, your chances of success will be tremendously enhanced. If you maintain a positive, attitude your significant other will also, and your relationship will not suffer as a result of your medical situation.

After Your Recovery

1. Document your symptoms for the rest of your life. Even though your case has been closed, it might be reopened again if your disability returns and you haven't accepted a cash settlement. If the same area of your body becomes disabled, it may be considered a direct relationship to the original injury, a casual relationship, or a completely new injury. Your doctor and the Workers' Compensation doctor will decide.

2. Visit your primary physician periodically, at least every six months, to monitor your physical condition, to document any residual symptoms you are experiencing, and to obtain prescriptions for medications. Send reports to the Workers' Compensation insurance carrier assigned to your case.

3. Keep a diary of the days you experience pain, the location of the pain, the intensity on a scale of 1-10, the time of day, and what (if anything) caused the pain.

4. Know your limitations and don't exceed them. If you know you shouldn't do something, don't do it. Don't push yourself beyond your new limits. Maybe you used to be able to lift 50 pounds, but now you can only lift 15 pounds. If you try to do what you did before the accident you will probably end up in the hospital, in surgery, or worse. It's not worth it. Get someone to help you or perform the task for

you.

5. Concentrate on getting well. Exercise, eat right, control your weight, and try to avoid aggravating the injury or relapsing your illness. The best way to win at Workers' Compensation is to stay healthy, so you don't need it.

6. Take medication only as prescribed and only as needed. Don't let yourself get addicted to powerful painkillers or muscle relaxers. Try not to take medications for very long periods if you can avoid it. Many medications have adverse side effects and react with other drugs including alcohol.

Social Security Disability Benefits

If you are totally disabled, you are probably eligible for Social Security Disability Benefits. Contact your local Social Security Administration and complete the necessary forms to apply for benefits.

Protecting Yourself – A Word of Warning

Private investigators are often hired by state insurance carriers and retirement officials. They spy on people who may be lying to get workers' compensation or disability pension benefits. Working undercover, using remote control cameras and "pinhole" cameras mounted in their baseball caps, private investigators acquire evidence that prevents applicants from getting Workers' Compensation benefits.

Documented cases include the following four employees with back injuries who had filed for workers compensation claims and were supposedly unable to work. They were videotaped by private investigators performing tasks that they claimed to be unable to perform at work. One was filmed lifting a keg of beer from the trunk of his car. The second was filmed driving his fishing boat out on a lake. A third individual was filmed loading sheets of plywood into a truck. And a fourth was videotaped bending at the waist and pulling weeds in his yard. All four lost their Workers' Compensation benefits. (Tampa Tribune, January 30, 1994)

If you have a legitimate injury or illness that prevents you from working, don't take advantage of the time off by trying to do work around the house. Follow your doctor's advice and rest, without any physical activity other than walking. You are probably extremely bored from the inactivity and may think you feel good enough to do a little work around the house. You undoubtedly have some powerful painkillers in your medicine cabinet in case you strain the weakened muscles and joints. You may work slowly, carefully, and take frequent breaks; but a private investigator might make a video of you resulting in a loss of your benefits. It isn't worth the risk. Ask a friend or hire a professional to do the work.

Related References

- The National Institute for Occupational Safety and Health (NIOSH) operates programs in every state to improve the safety and health of workers. It offers statistics on injuries and deaths on the job and costs by state. Employers can receive information specific to their occupational health or safety problems. You can also phone them at 800-356-4674.

- Bureau of Labor Statistics Safety and Health Statistics offers statistics by costs, injuries, illnesses, and fatalities. You'll also find demographic and industry information. You can also phone them at (202) 691-6199.

- Occupational Safety and Health Administration (OSHA) outlines steps for an employer to take to protect their employees from work-related hazards. Employers with more than 11 employees are required to maintain and post logs for job-related injuries. States with OSH programs can receive up to 50% of its program operating costs from OSHA. You can also phone them at 800-321-6742.

My Personal Experience

This section of the book contains information regarding the forms, documents, letters and other data from my own experience with a work-related injury. Perhaps they will help you to document your case and be successful. I have a four-inch, 3-ring binder bulging with paperwork about my injury and Workers' Compensation claims. Like any government agency, Workers' Compensation will bury you with forms and paperwork containing important details that you cannot ignore or overlook. Read everything they send you, front and back. You will also receive lots of paperwork from the Workers' Compensation insurance carriers. My employer kept changing insurance carriers, so I had to deal with three different insurance companies. It can be very confusing and overwhelming. I think they may deliberately make it that way to wear you down and scare you into submission. I also had another insurance company from my bank that paid my car loan payments while I was unable to work.

I eventually was ruled permanently, partially disabled. I still experience pain and limitations from by back injuries, even though it has been many years since my first work-related injury. Workers Compensation insurance still pays for any related expenses such as medication, surgeries, and doctor visits that I require. I still write to them regularly and remind them that I exist and I continue to experience the effects of my injury.

When I was injured, I did not give up and flush my life down the drain. My doctor said I could not return to my old job because it involved physical labor and heavy lifting. I repeatedly re-injured myself, aggravated the original back injury, and spent weeks unable to work and in rehabilitation. So, I returned to college and finished my two-year degree while working full time. Then I enrolled in a four-year college and got my Bachelor's Degree. I was fortunate because I qualified for Veteran's Educational Benefits. I often had to request a more comfortable chair so that I could endure an entire class. Sometimes I had to carry a heating pad with me, sit by an electrical outlet, plug it in and place it in the small of my back during classes. Many times I couldn't sit at all, and I had to stand in the back of the room during the lecture. It took me ten years to complete my entire education because I attended evening classes. But, my education was my ticket to change jobs and stay employed. I now work at a desk job, so I don't have to do any heavy lifting.

You need to think of your future and how you can break the cycle of injury and disability. You may need to change jobs, go back to school, or move to a warmer climate. Cold weather makes my back ache worse, so I moved from a northern state to Florida. Do whatever you need to do to keep active, stay employed and be productive. It takes time, determination, and effort but it can be done. There is always a way.

Good luck to you.

Documenting the Initial Injury and Claim

NOTE: The form numbers and titles may vary from state to state.

Form C-2, Employer's Report of Injury – Worker's Compensation Board. This form is available from your employer and must be completed when you are injured to document the injury. Mail the form to the Worker's Compensation Board at the address provided.

Form C84.4, Notice to Claimant. This form, or a similar form, acknowledges that the Workers' Compensation Board received your form C-2 and assembled a file in connection with the injury you reported.

Form C11, Employers Report of Injured Employee's Change of Employment Status Resulting From Injury. This form is sent to the Workers' Compensation Board from your employer. It documents the injury and date, nature of the injury, days missed from work, the employer's address and insurance carrier.

Form C-6, Notice that the Payment of Compensation Has Begun Without Awaiting Award of the Workers Compensation Board. This form documents your injury, date of injury, address, insurance carrier, type of injury, weekly compensation pay, date disability began, date employer reported injury, date of carrier's receipt of employer's form, date first payment mailed, etc.

Statement of Rights

Form C430S, Workers' Compensation Board Statement of Rights. This form is provided to all new claimants and, in summary, states the following:

- All workers who are injured while working, or who suffer from an occupational disease, may be entitled to workers' compensation benefits.

- Unless your claim is minor, requiring no medical treatment and causing no time lost from work, you should file a claim for benefits within two years of the date you are injured or your right to benefits may be lost.

- You are entitled to compensation if your injury keeps you from work for more than seven days, compels you to work at lower wages, results in facial scarring, or results in permanent disability to any part of your body. You are entitled to necessary medical treatment even if you do not lose time from work.

- Obtain necessary medical treatment immediately. You are entitled to be treated by a physician, podiatrist or chiropractor of your choice if he or she is authorized by the Chairman, Workers' Compensation Board.

- Tell your doctor, hospital, or pharmacist to file reports with the Workers' Compensation Board and with your employer or your employer's insurance carrier.

- Do not pay your doctor or hospital. The insurance carrier will pay their bills if your case is not disputed. If your case is disputed, the doctor or hospital must wait for payment until the Board decides your case.

- You are also entitled to be reimbursed for drugs, crutches or any apparatus prescribed by your doctor and for car fare or other necessary expenses going to and from your doctor's office or the hospital. Get receipts for such expenses.

- You are not required to have anyone represent you in any worker's compensation proceedings, but you have the right to be represented by an attorney or licensed representative if you so choose. If you obtain representation, do not pay your attorney directly. When the Workers' Compensation Board rules on your case, the attorney's or representative's fee will be set by the Board and the amount will be deducted from your award.

- Go back to work as soon as you are able. Compensation payments are never as high as your wages.

- Your employer may not ask you to waive your right to compensation nor may your employer deduct any money from your pay to contribute to the payment of workers' compensation insurance premiums. You cannot be discharged or discriminated against for filing a claim for workers' compensation benefits.

Workers' Compensation Forms and Communications

Memorandum of Decision. This form is issued to the claimant, the claimant's employer, and any applicable insurance companies. It documents the decision of the Workers' Compensation Board. It may list several case numbers, cases closed, cases combined, cases re-opened, etc. It may list a payment of medical bills or prescription drug bills that you (the claimant) requested. It may also announce a 'final' decision, such as "claimant was classified permanent partial disability and case was continued." Average weekly pay may be stated as well.

Form C88, Acknowledgement of Correspondence or Request for Information. This form documents that the Workers Compensation office received your letter or other correspondence. It may request further information such as: "Please advise status of unpaid pharmacy bills referred to by Claimant in his letter dated x/x/xx."

Form C323, Attached bills in connection with above case are being forwarded for your prompt attention. This form is sent to a doctor, pharmacist, or hospital and the Claimant regarding unpaid bills related to the injury. It documents the case number, Claimant, date of accident or injury, and amount of money owed.

Form C-84.4, Notice to Claimant. This form can scare the life out of you. It may state that your case is controverted (disputed). A form C-6, C-7, or C-9 accompanies the form depending on whether they are not disputing your case and payment has begun, disputing your case and withholding payments, or not disputing your case but not yet issuing payments for reasons stated.

Form C-16, Notice of Trail Hearing. This form is issued to announce a hearing regarding your case. The form lists the date, time and location of the hearing. Also the usual case numbers, date of the accident, employer, claimant, insurance carriers, etc. The form also states the Claimant and carrier should be present and produce evidence and witnesses. The case will be decided on the evidence presented. There will be no adjournment except for good and sufficient cause. The issues to be discussed are listed at the bottom such as Accident, Notice, or Casually Related Disability.

Form C-8, Notice That Payment of Compensation for Disability Has Been Stopped or Modified. This form is issued when your payment amount is changed (rate adjusted) or when you are released by your doctor to return to work. The form provides dates that you received payments and dates when you returned to work, and payments stopped.

Form C-10, Notice of Preliminary Hearing. Very similar to form C-16, but for a preliminary hearing

Form C200, Motion Calendar Notice. The Workers' Compensation Board sends this form after a hearing. It states the decision of the Board and lists any awards that will be issued or other decisions of the Board. This form is your opportunity to formally reply, appeal, protest, or submit further evidence. The back of the form has an area where you can write your thoughts and return the form. If there are no further comments the action stated on the form will become final at the date of the hearing listed on the form

Form C-71, Report of Medical Examination. This form is issued by the Workers' Compensation doctor and states the nature and date of the injury, recommended continued treatment, results of his exam, and your classification, such as "permanent partial disability."

Form C-23, Notice of Decision. This form states the final decision of the Workers' Compensation Board. It may indicate something like "No new accident. Case closed and combined with file 123456789," or "Closed. No active medical treatment," or "Continued to next available calendar upon re-opening," or "permanent, partial disability."

Glossary

Adjournment - to postpone your hearing until a later time.

Alleged - a condition said to exist but not yet proven.

Carrier - the insurance company paying workers' compensation claims for your employer.

Claimant - the person filing a workers' compensation claim.

Compensation - payment as recovery for loss of wages and medical expenses.

Controvert - to deny a workers' compensation claim.

Day in Court - your legal right to defend your claim in court.

Deposition - oral or written questions asked of the claimant, under oath, outside of the courtroom. A transcript, recording, or word for word account, is made of the deposition.

Disability - loss of physical or intellectual ability that prevents a person from working.

Disability Compensation - payments made to an employee for the period of absence from work due to disability. Social Security and Workers' Compensation may provide disability benefits.

Disability Insurance - insurance coverage purchased to protect an employee's salaries during periods of disability.

Disability Retirement - a retirement plan which pays an employee's salary during total disability until normal retirement age, when standard retirement benefits take effect.

Disfigurement - an injury that deforms or affects a person's beauty, symmetry, or appearance.

Evidence - any proof (witnesses, records, documents, exhibits, concrete objects, etc.) which help support your claim and convince the court.

Expert Witness - a witness whose education or experience gives them specialized knowledge about a subject. A physician is an expert witness.

Industrial Disease - a physical disorder which is caused by one's occupation. An example is carpal tunnel syndrome.

Lay Witness - a secular, non-professional witness, such as someone other than a doctor.

Memorandum - an informally written document from the Workers' Compensation office.

Occupational Disease - a disease resulting from exposure to unhealthy substances during employment. Examples include black lung disease, asbestosis, and cancer.

Occupational Hazard - an accident or disease which is related to a specific occupation.

Occupational Safety and Health Act (OSHA) - federal law administered by the Occupational Safety and Health Administration to reduce on-the-job injuries, illnesses, and deaths among working men and women in the United States.

Pain and Suffering - a term used to describe the mental and emotional trauma associated with physical pain. Payment for pain and suffering is restricted by law in some states.

Partial Disability - unable to perform some portion of your job that you did before the accident.

Permanent Disability - unable to ever return to the work formerly performed before the accident, though this incapacity may be either total or partial.

Retainer - compensation paid in advance.

Temporary Disability - temporarily unable to work but expected to recover completely.

Total Disability - unable to perform any substantial part of ordinary duties, though still able to perform a few minor duties and be present in the place of employment.

Workers' Compensation Acts - state and federal laws enabling payment to employees, or their dependents, for employment-related accidents and diseases. To encourage employers to carry Workers' Compensation Insurance the Acts eliminate employees' rights to bring legal action directly against their employer.

Workers' Compensation Boards or Courts - the authoritative and legal organizations established to review Workers' Compensation cases in most states.

Workers' Compensation Insurance - insurance coverage

provided by employers or purchased by employees to cover risks under Workers' Compensation laws.

Our Other Books

Books written by Raymond Hall and/or Sharon Hall

Visit the Amazon website to order.

www.ingramcontent.com/pod-product-compliance
Lightning Source LLC
Chambersburg PA
CBHW030037230526
45472CB00002B/557